CODE DOMESTICITY

poems by

Dana Reeher

Finishing Line Press
Georgetown, Kentucky

CODE DOMESTICITY

Copyright © 2025 by Dana Reeher
ISBN 979-8-88838-925-6 First Edition

All rights reserved under International and Pan-American Copyright Conventions. No part of this book may be reproduced in any manner whatsoever without written permission from the publisher, except in the case of brief quotations embodied in critical articles and reviews.

ACKNOWLEDGMENTS

"A Festive Return to Normal" is a found poem from a photo caption from The Sharon Herald, 6/14/2021.

"Worst Shift" was previously published in the Fall 2022 issue of Intima: A Journal of Narrative Medicine.

"Dear Officer" was based on the following prompt: As of March 28, 2020, French citizens are required to print out a form explaining their motivation for leaving the house an hour a day. You carry this form to present to any police officer. On the form, you list 5 reasons for going out—this is your motivation. Going to a funeral is not allowed. Write, in the form of a letter, your motivation to leave the house. You must include 5 reasons. One must be one word. One must be absurd. One must be to acquire an object that you are going to use in a manner other than it was designed for.

"Plums" was inspired after "This is Just to Say" by William Carlos Williams and "The Conditional" by Ada Limon.

Thank you to my husband, Matt, for all his support with this project.

Publisher: Leah Huete de Maines
Editor: Christen Kincaid
Cover Art: CC0 Public Domain
Author Photo: Melanie Rae Buonavolonta
Cover Design: Elizabeth Maines McCleavy

Order online: www.finishinglinepress.com
also available on amazon.com

Author inquiries and mail orders:
Finishing Line Press
PO Box 1626
Georgetown, Kentucky 40324
USA

Contents

I
Ars Poetica: Scissors 1
Field Trip to My Grandfather's House 2
Immortality 3
Five Dollar Bill 4
Library 5
A Festive Return to Normal 6
Robot Nursing 7
Last We Ever Heard 8
Switch, Nest, Sleep, Repeat 9
Worst Shift 10
Remember the Time 11
Flowers 13
She Carried You 14
Room to Room 15
Strange Kid 16
Electronic and Print 17

II
Mascot 21
Conversation: Ex-Lover 22
Ode to My Laundry Basket 23
The Sweater Monologue 24
Pocket 26
Snowqueen 27
Eclipse 28
Strange Kid 2 (or Pain) 29
Dusty Lamp 30
Hoarder 31
Sweet Cherry 32
Scar 33
Imagination On My Tongue 34
Morning Coffee 35
10 Things to Do 36

III

The Eye of the Hare 39
Onion 40
Surfside 41
Dear Officer 43
Wildflower 44
Ars Poetica: Chickens and Turkeys 45
Ragdoll 46
The Arachnid 48
The Centipede 49
In the Instruction Lab, Nurses' Hospital 50
Plums 51
Insomnia 52
Lullaby on a Cold Winter Night 53
Mother Shadow 54
Wanting Everything to Move 55
Guillotine 56
Ars Poetica: Tesla 57
Stream 58
Arrest 59
Bees and Blackberries 60
Ocean 61
Baby Doll Does Too Much 62

Let Us play Yesterday— from #728 by Emily Dickinson

…*We will it so/ and so it is/ past all accident*—from *The Ivy Crown* by William Carlos Williams

I

Ars Poetica: Scissors

I am 3 years old, sitting on the linoleum under the plastic countertop. Trying to blend myself in shadows, taking my blue scissors and cutting my curly brown hair. I'm mingling with the shadows, potato bins and coffee beans. Mom finds me. Her face moves from worried to curious, surprised, to angry. She rips my blue scissors away and hides them: "You can't be trusted." But I'm creating something new, the curls look like feathers. I can make a bird of hair-feathers and I will be brand new.

Field Trip to My Grandfather's House

What is it about All Hallows' Eve,

the chill that opens the door

to another plane?

I see shadows

of my grandfather, smoking his cigar,

sitting in his tilt-back

and my grandmother scolding him,

chasing him outside

to the porch with his cigar.

I try to touch them, but they disappear

like tiny capillaries

I smell the tobacco and baby

powder cologne of my grandfather

and the stubble on his chin when he

kissed me goodbye, never aware

of the coming extinction.

Immortality

"Immortality is such a strong word," she thought continuing her push-ups and jumping jacks. "But this is why I'm exercising, to get closer to holy immortality and further from mortality. We all know what happens to *mortals*— No one wants that, especially not me. I have too many things left to do, like writing a book, publishing a blog, building a homeless shelter for women, and having another child. I can't accomplish any of those if I'm dead. The only thing that matters— If I can get all of these done, then I will finally be able to rest." The whispers, a voice of persistence: "But think about what you could do next…." She grabs the towel from the metal bar, and starts chin-ups, composing songs aloud of her own design.

Five Dollar Bill

"This $5 bill is meaningless," he shouts. "But it's all I have," she cries. "I can't believe you would pay me with paper money, it's so dirty," he says. She grabs the five, runs into cold moonlight as snowflakes fall on her face. The wind picks up, almost knocking her over, blowing the five from her hand. She runs after it. She won't be able to buy food for the week if it blows away. She chases, so focused on reaching the money she runs into a man walking down the street. "Watch where you're going!" and they both fall to the ground. "I'm sorry, I'm trying to get my last five back." "Five dollars won't get you very much these days," but he agrees to help her. They both spot it, as if held by invisible string. He pushes forward, reaches out, grabs the five, the first time since the city fell all those years ago that he has had paper money, much less a five, in his hands. Though he knows she needs it, he can't help but wonder what he could get—milk or cheese? Fresh loaf of bread? Fresh fruits and vegetables?

Now, most transactions accumulated debt, which you then had to work off by the end of the 24-hour period. He knew the five would be valued in the marketplace. Maybe she hadn't noticed that he grabbed the money and then could keep it. She breaks him from his thoughts: "Oh thank you for getting my five." Scowling, he hands it to her. "Let me repay you. Even though this is my last five, I'll buy you something you need." Surprised, he agrees to her proposition and suggests a triple-iced mocha with 7 shots of neon green syrup, his favorite drink.

Library

Library books unfurl in the air while I attempt to put them away. They fly off the cart and onto the shelves.

Years ago, I had to hand-shelve all the books on my own. I taught people how to use the microfilm machine to look at old newspaper clips: their grandparents were married or their great grandparents died. Pulling the past month's newspapers (all 30) was a joy—newsprint inched up over my arms and hands, heavy papers all around. Magazines from 5 years back, with silver fish crawling and eating the books stored from 1883.

Now toys line shelves, hamsters in cages, a turtle in an aquarium. But the librarians and library users are all the same. I go in, at random, unable to enjoy myself, reordering the books according to their Dewey classification—150.08 *You and Your Self-Esteem,* 616.2 365 *Days to Better Health* and in my intoxicating reorganizing, hear "Hello—I haven't seen you do that for so long—do you still work here?" My startled reply always "no." I return to reordering (550.01 Cosmos) and notice the turtle has escaped the aquarium and is dripping water on the shelves and picture books. Turtle crawls toward the giant art landscape books, thick grass like carpet under each foot, climbs into 720.92 *The life and works of Frank Lloyd Wright*— turns, smiles, clasps my hand, carries me with him.

A Festive Return to Normal
 —*photo caption from* The Sharon Herald, *6/14/2021*

The three-day festival

became one of the first

local events

to return after a year

without fun

without parties

without lines of people

drinking beer, standing on top

of each other, shaking hands,

eager to move hips, legs, feet

to the drumming,

guitar strumming,

tambourine rattling,

screaming off-key vocals,

of local bands

while a lone mask

blows by in the wind.

Robot Nurse

There once was a robot who was a nurse. The human nurses were not ready, of course. Every human went crazy and was also called lazy, because the robot could work at 1000 times the speed. The human nurses conversed with patients, gave hugs, patted wounds. The robots inflated blood pressure cuffs on patient arms until the cuffs exploded and arms flew off, like Barbie doll arms, landing outside the hospital, fingers pointed towards the sky, a warning. The human nurses reprogrammed the robots with sleep.exe, but the robots started echoing: "system error system error" until their default settings restored, then the cycle of blood pressure cuffs exploding and arms flying started again....

Last We Ever Heard

"That was the last we ever heard of him," she noted. "Darn it! I missed the whole story. What am I supposed to tell my children about their father's disappearance? I can only remember that he always told me, 'My skin was like a dried rotten onion—flaky and no good to eat.' But why would he say that? Context? Situation? I can't seem to recall any of it. Every day I keep losing pieces of him, bit by bit, until I can barely remember his name…something with a 'J' or a 'G'…. Geoff! That's what it was! Thank goodness I remembered—who knows what next…. Wait, are you here again and why?

Switch, Nest, Sleep, Repeat

The light flicks on, the wolf spider sits on the wall.

She screams, tries to squish it,

but it scurries behind the mirror.

She hits the mirror quickly—one, two, three—

to force the spider out of hiding.

It sneaks out below the mirror

onto the counter, near the sink.

The mirror falls,

shatters into a million shards

revealing a nest of babies,

unborn.

She finds a shoe, squashes the mother,

snatches its children and pitches them.

She doesn't notice that one

tiny spider crawled

under her skin and created

a new nest,

baby spiders waiting

until she lies down to sleep.

Worst Shift

The worst shift starts before you ever get to work, phone ringing, work calling to say "you're late" and you realize you shut your alarm instead of hitting snooze.

The worst shift starts when you arrive 30 minutes later without a cup of coffee. You realize your assignment includes the sickest patients on IV blood pressure meds and a patient in restraints who keeps trying to take his ventilator tubing from his mouth.

Your worst shift ever includes trading away your patients to receive a brand-new one ill with a virus untreatable by conventional methods. The patient is in isolation, so each time you enter the room, you must wear a paper gown, gloves, an N95 mask, and a face shield.

You are trying to communicate with the patient's family but can't because they are deaf and you don't know sign language and the translator is too scared to come in to the hospital and the translation device available doesn't include American Sign Language as an option. You finally communicate via written notes.

When you are trying to care for your patient, giving multiple blood pressure-sustaining medications and rotating the patient on their stomach to allow effective breathing and when you attempt to give shift report bedside to the oncoming shift, when the patient's heart stops and they stop breathing, and monitors alarm loudly. You start CPR and the code team takes forever to enter, all extra PPE unavailable.

Your worst shift ends when your patient dies despite your best attempts to save them.

Arriving home, 2 hours after your shift ended and you realize you have a fever… and are likely infected with the same virus. You worry, then sleep and then wake up, your coworkers staring down at you, now the patient, breathing in and out along with a ventilator in the ICU where you work; rolling from side to side, moving your arms and legs as if in slow-motion in a dream, when you suddenly sit straight-up in bed, coughing, gagging, gasping for air, beeping alarms, shouts of "Code Blue" echoing in your ears.

Remember the Time

the water got shut off because we forgot
to pay the enormous bill?
But you knew what to do,
how to take care of us—buying
water and using hand sanitizer and phoning
the water company every day.

Remember the time
I wanted to drink 20 pints of Guinness
because I thought we were going
to miss visiting Blarney Castle?
But you knew
exactly how to navigate to get us
there and back to Dublin.

Remember
you laid the mattresses and blankets
on the floor so we could have a bed
in our first tiny house?
The mattresses were more comfortable than the floor
and the blankets were warmer with you beside me.

The time
you got sick with the flu
all you could do was lie on the couch?
But I made you an appointment
to get a script for Tamiflu
and made you grilled cheese sandwiches
and soup until you felt better.

Remember the time
you made us pancakes and sausage for dinner
and you were so busy yelling "GOAL!" about the Pens game
you burnt the skillet?
We both had to scrub it,
but I was the one who
finally was able to get it clean.

Flowers

        They are

too beautiful,

too extraordinary

floating in and out of reality

with me. Yellow and orange

roses won't cure

Mrs. Smith's lung cancer.

There are no rosebuds

to entertain my senses.

I don't want flowers

In my life. They leave

when Mrs. Smith does, drifting from

location to location, like I do,

sharing hospital rooms.

She Carried You

That sunny winter day filled in a matter of minutes. She was in the semi-lit room with the ultrasound and was bluntly told you were dead then left alone with your image burned in her eyes and left on the screen in front of her, while waiting ages for the doctor to confirm.

But she never miscarried, she carried you the whole time, though she was unaware of your presence until it was already gone. She carried you until they forced your tiny, fragile strawberry-sized body from her womb. She mourns you privately, internally. She doesn't dare hope for another fragile strawberry. Worries it will repeat because she's incapable of being a mother again, takes herself out of the mother equation with her living child to avoid becoming more like the cruel helicopter blades of her own mother, yet tries to carry you—reaches for a small cluster of red berries surrounded by crowns of saw-toothed, hairy green leaves—hopes for another you.

Room to Room

He stands in the silver

white and blue kitchen

from our first home,

spreading butter and

jam over his toast,

but he doesn't see.

He walks from room

to room in our house through his day

but doesn't see me.

I ruffle his hair.

He sighs, laughs.

We sit together at the antique

maple dining room table and

he stares as if he can see me,

reaches for my hand, fades

before our hands meet.

Strange Kid

Barely noticing how fast she is moving, she notices the air becomes thinner making it easier to fly, but harder to breathe. "I just want to do what I want, and you can't make me do anything I don't want to do!" She recalls from her lessons at school, learned in secret "Slow breaths, keep moving, slow down your breathing."

She does as lesson and memory command, feeling both enraged and courageous, unfurls her large angel wings from her back rising above the clouds, watching Earth fall away from her—stars glide beneath her, feels wind blow in her face, over and under her body, through her hair, wings flapping without conscious thought—to soar above, below clouds and stars.

Electronic and Print

There were never enough books. Stacks were on chairs and under tables, bookshelves overflowing with books, alphabetized by title, separated by fiction, non-fiction, and poetry. She always wanted more, though many were left unread or half-read. She used the library—both the electronic and print, and that would help calm her fire, her need. But there were still times she found herself at 3am perusing online indie bookstores and even amazon.com to find another book she could procure and add. Would she ever be able to stop? Imagine a world with nothing but books around her, but what would become of her book collection after she died?

II

Mascot

All dressed up and ready for the spotlight.

Everyone knows who I am

when I have my costume on.

Crowds cheer when I walk into the stadium.

Adults and kids try to hug me and take pictures.

I'm dressed as your favorite mascot

from the baseball game—ketchup bottle!

After my performance, I take my costume off.

Need escape.

No one knows who I am.

I walk out to voices chattering, yelling.

Now I'm just another face smirking

through a sea of smirking faces,

avoiding contact until

the crowd thins, faces disappear,

mountains rise, a river rushes before me,

I breathe deeply again in solitude.

Conversation: Ex-Lover

Two women bump into each other while in a doctor's office waiting room.

You look familiar.

    Really?
    I just have a familiar face.

Do you know Nicholas and Jamie? Or Karl?

    Not really sure. Maybe Karl?

Oh, okay, Karl. I thought you looked familiar. He's my fiancé.

    Oh congratulations. He's a great guy.

Thanks.

    Did he tell you that we dated?

    That we used to fuck everyday in his giant Amish-made bed?

    That he said he wished he hadn't met me because he loved me, but felt committed to someone else, **his** ex-lover, who he was still in love with, even though she had a problem with prescription drugs.

    Did he tell you he loved the way I was able to interact with his boys— and his balls? That he wanted to commit to me but couldn't. That he just was having fun at first but found out I was more "marriage material" or "wife material" and not "just having fun" material, so he had to break it off, had to stop seeing me (but still wanted to fuck me).

I'm not sure, but I don't think he ever mentioned you.

Ode to My Laundry Basket

Thank you, oh sexy and square laundry basket, for holding dirty and clean clothes, they can be washed and folded and put away in closets and drawers. Thank you for holding the satin silkiness of day of the week underwear and smelly gym socks from tumbling on the floor gathering lint, dust, and hair. Thank you for keeping them in a space where they can be kept safe, the sacred space of clean laundry waiting to be folded. Thank you for staying atop the dryer, in the little closet you call home, your luscious frame ready.

The Sweater Monologue

I've dreaded this day since I picked you out of the thrift store. I would NEVER
wear something like you, your red worst of all colors—anger, heat, passion
and your colorful squares splattered across your front. Shades of blue,
purple, green, yellow, orange, teal, lime green in no particular order
    whatsoever.
Sighing, I pull you over my head, a signal that we are journeying and "trying
    something new."
How scratchy my skin is already at your touch. Am I that sensitive? Are you
    that irritating?
Whatever. I do notice a softness to your fabric that tempers the irritation.
Do I need to notice this about life (in general)? Or maybe it's just a crazy idea,
maybe that's why no one ever takes me seriously, because
they already know—I'm just a crazy-writer-trying-to-be-a-poet.
My husband, with his carved wooden spoon collection, has already noticed
    I'm wearing you.
Today is GREAT so far! After lunch, I teach undergraduate nursing students.
    None of them talk,
I'm certain because they are so taken aback by the brilliance of your color
    scheme,
but probably more likely because they are sleeping while they are supposed
to be attending class synchronously using Microsoft Teams. Or
maybe they are having intercourse, I read a social media post on Facebook
recently that surveyed students and found 10% of them were having
    intercourse
during class meeting times. Maybe I should start requiring them to
have their cameras on at all times. No, too much bandwidth will slow
the streaming. I can't even consider about how long it will take to upload
THAT video and don't even get me started on the IT services
(or should I say, lack thereof) at school. I feel like I could do a better job
and I have no formal IT training.
Is this sweater loading IT programs in me, like smart.exe or stupid.exe?
My daughter noticed you when she got home from school and I didn't say you
    were horrible—
maybe I'm becoming accustomed to your ugliness?
Are you growing on me? Oh dear, another complicated relationship,
not something that I need right now. Too many are "complicated,"
even the ones that shouldn't be. It's because I'm emotionally broken
into so many fragments, I can't be put back together the same way—

twice, three, or four times, like the splattering of your colors.
I accidentally spilled spaghetti sauce on the lime green colored square of the sweater.
I'm sure you barely noticed, but I noticed
the sauce. My daughter dropped her full fork of food on the floor and more sauce splattered onto
your purple-colored square. I admit I am not pleased, but find it sort of funny.
After dinner, while everyone else is watching television, I keep feeling your red color seeping
into my DNA, because I feel restless, like I need to be working or doing something
instead of mindlessly sitting like a potato. I try grading online
student assignments, but my attention wanders from assignments
to *The Big Bang Theory,* to cat videos my daughter is watching,
then to emails from students with questions about assignments and grades.
My brain is fried, maybe your red color is somehow frying my brain,
sending more electricity through every neuron until my brain
lights up like a firework and causes my home life to explode?
Or more likely, infiltrating my brain,
like many ideas, thoughts, and opinions, to the point in which
I feel I don't know who I am anymore. I don't know how to
have fun anymore— I forgot that skill somewhere along the path to
achieving my goals and ambitions, I guess.
Finally, this day has ended, and I peel you off. Look at all these little red spots on my arms from
scratching at you. At least now I can throw on my favorite worn-out Foo Fighters t-shirt and
climb into bed.

Pocket

My hand dips into his back pocket,

revealing we are walking together,

in tandem.

Moving, slowly,

each of my steps—right, left, right, left

mimics his—left, right, left, right,

an Earth-mirror of my path. His hand falls

into my back pocket and we rise,

legs rowing through the dark sky

like oars moving through water

squalls of snow, splashes of sunbursts,

moving right, left, right,

ready to follow trails of stars.

Snowqueen

The frost touches first. Rigidity through her knuckles, hands, wrists. She notices the paleness in the reflection of her younger sister's eyes. The hardness in her fingers grows, shifts to every joint, making them incapable of movement. She breathes, but feels her breath catch in her chest, a heaviness overtakes her torso. *Help!* but all that emerges is a soft whisper. She tries to run, but her legs and feet are like rocks—toes bone stones. She swallows hard, but her Adam's apple gets stuck in her throat. She looks down—she's turning into an icy diamond just like her older sister and mother foretold years before, Orion's ring on her hand. She is frozen in place.

                                            The hypothermia rises, adding a silvery shimmer to her skin, reminiscent of her white blood cells, similar to those of water and snowflakes—she hears water speaking to her now: *You have control, move your fingers back and forth, create snow and ice.* She feels her heart thumping, slower, glacializing in her chest, as her vision turns the fuzz gray of a broken cathode ray tube in a TV set—just as her snow blanket begins to cover the ground on her command.

Eclipse

The soothsayer shared predictions with a curse toward my companions and adversaries—hexing them with living for infinity and repeating the phrase "I have infinity" to every person coming into the light of their view. "I have infinity" rings through the air as the FedEx man waltzes by delivering packages. His stomach is empty, so I fill his plate from my fingertips with potatoes, steak, and green beans. The eclipse starts slowly, making the obvious obscure, and the shadows viewable in a heavenly orbit. A problem remains, though, as the fortune teller never revealed who has infinity. So now I'm asking—is it you?

Strange Kid 2 (or Pain)

She scrubs off green and gold paint, removes bobby pins, shards of glass, writhes in shackles that tie her down, cut into her soft skin. She struggles to release herself from this dark prison. She shakes, then finally gathers all her strength and unfurls her wings—the force, the heaviness, the *whoosh* of her wings breaks the shackles, freeing her and allowing her to soar skyward and become one with the sky and clouds. Coasting above the purple trees, she darts past pebbles and rocks thrown at her from the earth below, gliding over and under purple tree branches restricting her flight path toward promise in a vertical horizon.

Dusty Lamp

Dust and rust are forming in tiny corners, cling to the curves of my dust-bunny body, untouched for so long. Electricity runs through me and I remain plugged into the energy of the house, but my light and shade never illuminate. No one flips my switches. No one powers me on any longer. I watch LED lights turn on and off through my days, but my incandescence remains dark, unable to beam on the marble, stone, and oak table underneath—when my light burns, I see forgotten childhood toys, cake crumbs waiting to be picked up.

Hoarder

While you were busy screwing around with another lover,

I decided to find something for myself. You always said I

was lucky not to have my mind raped or polluted

by pornography. Instead, I filled it with the trash of our lives:

buttons, papers from our daughter's school,

pens, pencils, towels, blankets, books, notebooks half-filled

with notes from another time. All of these things, collecting

in the space you told me was mine.

Until I evacuated it all from our lives.

Standing in the kitchen,

washing dishes in blood, cleaning off my sins,

like the sin of your murder not murder.

Death hangs in the air, unseen by human eyes,

with your hands, small as rain drops, you grabbed the scythe,

unknowingly—

destroying your life

as blood drains out of you, back to me.

Sweet Cherry

I want to quit you, but can't. I keep jumping in for more every time I think I've had just enough. Your sweet cherry-ish taste, fizzy bubbles that splash on my face, I long for the touch of your taste on my tongue all day and all night. They tell me you're no good for me, but you're better than online shopping, collecting stamps, or chewed gum. Why won't the condemning eyes and faces let me have this one

delicious   taste

Scar

I know you, your roughness with smooth edges. The way you divide my thumb with a vertical slant, that day when I was 4 or 5 and stuck my thumb in the spinning spoke of a stationary bike. The spoke kept spinning, drew me in, made me want to touch it and run my thumb against it. Blood snuck out of my thumb, dripping down my hand and wrist, onto the wood floor, creating a puddle. Suddenness of getting into the car, holding a beige washcloth over my thumb, while I slid back and forth in the back seat, twisting with every curve to the hospital and doctor, who said I was <u>this close</u> to "needing stitches" (whatever that meant, I'm not a piece of clothing after all), and wrapped bandages slowing the puddles of red into drips of paint.

Imagination On My Tongue

I know you, old friend. I know your dark and your light, causing me to wake with fear and delight. You've fed many of my favorite fantasies and anxieties. From dinner with Benedict Cumberbatch and Phil Kessel to flies and ladybugs coming out of the showerhead. You've helped me wish on a unicorn horn—hitting the winning serve in a high-school volleyball game, publishing an article in *The New York Times* at age 25—all beyond my wildest beliefs.

Morning Coffee

Up, slowly, descend. Recite the alphabet backwards down each creaky step, hear the whoosh, feel the rush of cold water as it touches your hand in droplets falling from the spout. Hear the water sigh as it heats, then rushes with the bubbling water then the slow, then fast drip drip drip of coffee into the pot. Smell the fresh brew, so strong you can already taste it in your parched mouth. Percolation persists, until the pot sighs again and gives a small whistle signaling ready. Pour a cup into your favorite mug, "ding ding" your spoon on the side to ensure every last drop makes it into the cup after you've added cream and sugar. The extra "ting" when the spoon softly lands on countertop while newsprint and coffee the flavor of midnight dance over pages, telling tales of local life.

10 Things to Do

>   —After Ted Berrigan "10 Things I Do Everyday"

I

Get born

Drink from breasts, bottles

Eat sushi for breakfast in Tokyo

Learn to curse in Mandarin

II

Sleep in till noon

Play "Go Fish"—500 times with my daughter

Wonder if my mom is still taking her medication

Worry about getting my family sick

Read my daughter a bedtime story and kiss her goodnight

Feel guilty for not doing more today

Fall into dreamless sleep

III

Resume Starbucks—but only the drive-thru

Worry about my daughter going to kindergarten (in person?)

Play with her out in the sandbox—every day for the last 300

Observe people wearing masks—correctly—incorrectly

Stay distant from mom so she won't get sick

IV

Wear a mask each time I go out,

frustrated by the unmasked trying to talk to me at the grocery store

Clean the house

Watch the news only when necessary

III

The Eye of the Hare

Evasive maneuvers, racing in and out of the shadowy bushes and flowers,

I am trying to catch the white tail, long ears, and big amber eyes of the hare.

Solitary by nature, long hind legs carry them away,

furry writhing flesh when I catch them,

eyes gazing upwards towards the moon.

They continue to rustle in the brush and leaves, noisy

yet invisible to me, scuttling off

waving their white tails in defiance.

The moon continues to rise, leaves whish through the air,

creating images of owls flying high above the clouds.

The hare, zipping around, mocks me like a dog at a track,

in pursuit. I pitch once more,

methodically, abandoning all hope

but like a rubber band bouncing back into shape,

I decide to try again to attract the eye of the hare.

Onion

Peel back the layers

with your strong, muscular hands.

Your fingertips, stained yellow

from too many cigarettes, work hard

to remove skins and flesh—This is the only time

I've ever seen you cry—Delicately,

ever so softly, your

hands pull back that first layer,

only to find more layers,

stinging your blue eyes with tears.

Your yellow fingertips wipe tears

and streams from your soft-stubbled face.

The onion laughs, full of more.

Surfside

I watch from the beach house window,

reaching for the silver wedding ring

you left on the driftwood dresser

the night you willingly floated off

and sank to the bottom of the sea.

"Humans' stupidity is only eclipsed by their laziness,"

she shouts. Her eyes, blue

like the Caribbean in June, project calm,

a feeling she cannot possess with her

thirst for truth and choice and

"socio reengineering provides deceptions

and a swirling vortex of terror"

A gathering of gulls

sit nonchalant outside the enclosed back porch

flying, stalking for human food,

then soaring ahead of the squabble

crashing into the castles in the clouds

at sunset, destroying the beachfront

paradise they call home.

She shouts like a lunatic

then cowers under her cloak,

soothsayer, schizophrenic,

she is a luminous phenomenon that continues

to walk the earth, the sea,

in search of liberation.

Dear Officer:

Please allow this woman to:

        Touch,

        burn in the atmosphere.

        Hear the colors of the trees.

        Taste puffy white clouds.

        See heavy metal music.

        Smell sunlight.

Such a small request could not possibly lead

to an arrest during social isolation.

Sincerely,

A Woman in Waiting

Wildflower

She paces, expectant

wondering if the thin

line will change

her world, blue

line, clouds pass,

warm air blows

Yes or no?

holds the answer

Blue line wildflowers

pass the open,

hold the open

window answer.

Ars Poetica: Chickens and Turkeys

Once, while growing up on a farm, a little girl helped to take care of the cows, chickens, turkeys, and horses. On this ordinary day, the little girl noticed that the chickens and turkeys seemed to have grown. She crept closer while they were eating their feed, and suddenly, she was looking a chicken right in the eye, as if a Velociraptor had come to life! The soft feathers, colored brown, yellow, red, and white nearly covered her body. The girl didn't worry about getting her eyes pecked out, though the chickens and turkeys were 4 feet tall—like she was right now! Her shoes felt looser, but her pants felt too tight. She wanted to ask mom if she was growing but decided to wait. Besides, if she kept growing, did that mean they would keep growing too? And what caused them to become that large to begin with? Was it something she did? She let the chickens peck peck peck the feed out of her hands without worrying about the chickens and turkeys thoughts.

Ragdoll

Her boss compares her

to Jim. "You and Jim have so much

potential, but Jim works harder."

In the conference room, Jim

knocks over his coffee, spilling all

over her reports.

She believes

purposeful. Jim

gets promoted. Jim

says "You might get promoted...but I'm first of course."

Jim starts giving her menial tasks.

"Fix this report for me, I just don't have time."

Like a wet rag

she drags herself across the floor

daily. She's told "You must

write 15 articles by December for a raise."

She heads back to her cubicle.

Her file folders are arranged in color order.

She removes them all, throwing them onto her desk, re-organizing

them in reverse color order.

She notices Jim in the staff break room, laughing and drinking coffee.

She continues to observe him after everyone else leaves the room.

She watches as Jim takes 7 vanilla flavored coffee creamers and sticks them in his pants pocket.

He takes time to add hot water to the already old pot of coffee,

and as a finale,

spits in it, adds a sprinkle of pencil shavings and lint from his shirt

stirs the pot vigorously, before returning to his cubicle.

The Arachnid

looks for the next delicious insect. Red

markings on the black arachnid's back, designed to warn prey

of the poison inside. Enough to kill an insect—or a human.

Delicate web, silken and sleek, hums with an earthy tone.

A fly caught in the web stirs, struggling to escape, survive.

The arachnid ventures, crawling in to kill. The fly attempts to flee,

bounces off the smooth rocks below, then soars.

The Centipede

I walk quietly,

waiting for my bitter brew

percolating.

I feel a tickle over my toes,

but brush it away without

a thought, prepare my coffee.

Again, my toes,

this time I glance down.

I give a small shriek,

A centipede!

My   kitchen   5 am!

the last time

I saw this type of creature,

years ago, disguised

as cousin Jake, inched

over me, touching sacred

spaces with tiny legs,

to invade my home.

In the Instruction Lab, Nurses' Hospital

I can't stop remembering the things you ask me to forget—the way you pointed and laughed when I spoke to you or when you lay in bed naked all day and didn't come to class. Or how you yell for no apparent reason, or you roll your eyes and flip your hair when told it's YOUR responsibility to learn information, that you need to learn how to think critically, not just regurgitate information back. Your patients are not going to have the answers, you will be expected to know what to do. No one is going to do it for you.

Plums

Say the plums weren't cold,

say the stone fruits weren't delicious,

say the plums weren't in the icebox,

would you still have eaten them?

Say I didn't forgive you,

say I expected to eat them and the plums were the only things I could eat.

Or say the purple apricots weren't for me at all?

What if I had been saving them for you and you ate them anyway?

At least you didn't eat the strawberries, tart yet sweet, so juicy, dribbling

down my chin, staining my white shirt and jeans with little red spots.

Say I had eaten the plums and the strawberries and left you with none.

Would you have forgiven me?

I probably wouldn't have asked for your forgiveness anyway, but say I did?

Would you have cared or noticed that I ate plums and strawberries for

breakfast?

Say breakfast doesn't matter at all,

say we just enjoy the fruit that we have now.

Insomnia

Dust on the spiderwebs,
    ceiling fan, irregularities
        of each speck in the zzzzz of my spouse
            dreaming sports or sex tonight   Pet Spooky
                a million times she dreams climbing trees catching birds
Brush my teeth on the neighbor's
    dead tree stumps   Leftover from when he murdered
        "sick" trees   Urinate 10 times   Walk slowly down the stairs, alphabet
            letter every step: "A apple, B bear, . . ." like the remainder
of an old childhood

Rhyme sticks on the steps,
    brown carpet hides wood and screws
forming the staircase
Couch, avoid TV, eating crunchy
    nut butter on graham   Could these sandwiches
pass for a meal at any other time of day,
    back up stairs recite alphabet back-
wards Z zebra, Y yo-yo . . . Dream
a night's sleep
        sunrise
            write a poem

Lullaby on a Cold Winter Night

Hush now, my child.

Listen to the calico cat

in the hall meow for its kibble.

Listen to the beat

of Mozart's symphonies

in your head.

Bright blue eyes

blink from

wakefulness to sleep,

brown curls slip

onto your flushed face.

Snowflakes fall

outside your window,

covering the dark

pasture with a blanket

revealed only

by moonlight's

sparkling diamonds.

Mother Shadow

                Directed

toward work, no compromise,

on a power trip because of her role,

providing extra cash for her personal library

while simultaneously beating herself up

for missing her daughter's recitals,

she must climb,

              provide,

no one else can

take care of her

or her daughter.

              Her spirit dulls,

turns spidery, falling into washing dishes, folding laundry

until she finds she can't get out of bed. She

sleeps until the next day, then arises, finds

strength in creating playlists

of music on her iPhone to avoid changing

the radio dial, while critiquing

her daughter's every decision.

Wanting Everything to Move

Any step you take is like an earthquake that rattles my entire floor world to the roots. When you walk over me, it's as if a tornado has blown thru, moving everything around, including me. As a speck of dust, I sit and wait for everything to move around me, not for me to move everything. I dreamily float around once I am moved, undetected by anyone, landing on the windowsill, watching flowers outside blossom and bloom.

Guillotine

The queen

raises her

guillotine

over and over

at her jester husband

for not delivering a sperm

creating another daughter.

The rapidity

with which she slices

at her role and jester

gives a rhythm,

each head dropping on

command as she refuses

submission to those who believe

they should give the commands.

Ars Poetica: Tesla

I never had to ask, it was personalized, which accelerated my solitude. I discovered I could write while the car drove anywhere and everywhere and could loop around for hours and no one would interrupt me, allowing my poetic transformation.

Later as I stepped into the car, peals of laughter from outside the car burst from my husband, and the singing of Christmas carols (in July) by my daughter echo in my ears. My commute becomes my escape, the only time I could spend writing.

While writing, my elbow accidentally pushes a small button. Mechanical wings grow out from the doors and a small jet pack appears at the tail and I take off toward the horizon, just like my poem.

Stream

I remember going to the water, riding my bike, leaning it next to an oak. The trickling sound of the current as it flows by. Rough tree bark in my soft hands, tall flowers whip against my legs as I run by. Birds sing their afternoon songs in harmony with the water. Bees buzz past, rest on flowers, retrieve pollen for their hive.

Splash through the cold brook, smell dirt and uncut grass, catch a smooth salamander in my hand. Catch a flat frog in my hand, watch as he puffs his thin chest like a balloon at me while I watch the pulsing of his heart. See a rabbit hop two feet in front of me, like Alice, begging me to follow to another world of magic, danger, and intrigue. I curve in and out of the sun and shadows, find the path to a boulder. Climb the rock, realize I can see for miles, then sit atop and sing to butterflies, dance a jig on stones, and write poems in crevices.

Arrest

The first time

it was a mistake. She happened

to be near the pet store when the REAL THIEF

arrived and broke in. Of course,

she went in to make sure the animals were okay.

The thief had already robbed the store.

Seconds passed faster than she could count

and she heard the wailing sirens, the surprise

of cops freezing her to the ground. They

clamped the cold handcuffs

around her wrists, ignoring her screams.

She was 13 years old.

Eventually, the cops took her seriously and finally released her.

The second time,

she was in the right place. She had joined PETA

and was helping to release butterflies

from a greenhouse at the zoo.

The zookeepers had left the delicate pollinators

in wilting plants and flowers, cold air conditioning,

barely any nectar or pollen to eat.

Those butterfly like creatures in the zoo

should be first to taste freedom. Freeing

was her calling,

and if it meant arrest,

she was ready.

Bees and Blackberries

When he is a teen, my father takes time outside with his 6-year-old brother—leads him down the long dirt road to the blackberry patch bordering on the neighbor's backyard to teach him the proper way to pick them. While skinny and fat fingers pull berries, a swarm of bees attacks—my dad runs as fast as his long, lean body and legs will take him, but his brother, unable to keep up, is stung 75 times. My father is blamed for his younger brother's injuries, but let's be honest, did he know any better? He told jokes to help his brother feel better, but nothing more. Between the zeroes and ones of the events of their lives they both say: Error 404 File not found.

Ocean

I want to keep walking deeper and deeper until I'm enveloped below the crashing waves, flashes of light, waves leaping towards the sky, pulled back to earth by gravity. Waves topple boats, fragments of wood dive deep, landing on the bottom quiet. I want to swirl with current, sink touching the sand, first with my leaden feet, then with my head, emerge smooth as stones and sand. The sea's hand nets around my body, carrying me deep inside the tranquility below. I want to lay my body down, let the ocean drag me down and cover me with all the myths, lies, and debris I've created to elevate myself and stay afloat.

Baby Doll Does Too Much

Baby Doll thought she could wash the dishes and change the baby's diaper at the same time. She constantly bit off more than she could chew and blamed the stars and the time projects would take, but truthfully she thought she could do everything. Baby Doll knew she could attend two virtual meetings at once—that made her feel she could constantly multi-task with every aspect of her life. Baby Doll was only able to pay partial attention to her life and missed seeing her sisters at Thanksgiving dinners; her daughter's soccer, baseball, and basketball games; coffee with friends. Baby Doll wanted to remedy this problem but wasn't certain where to let go—she liked being part of so many different activities and didn't want to choose what should stay and what should go.

Dana Reeher, born in Pittsburgh, Pennsylvania, is a poet, nurse practitioner, and adjunct professor. She has also been published in I*ntima: A Journal of Narrative Medicine, Voices from the Attic Volume XXVII, and YWCA Women's Art Show: 40 poets for 40 years.* She graduated from Carlow University's Master of Fine Arts in Creative Writing program with a poetry specialization in May 2022. She is also a member of the Madwomen in the Attic community-based writing workshops affiliated with Carlow University. She earned a PhD in nursing from University of Phoenix in 2018, and a Master of Science in Nursing with Family Nurse Practitioner specialization from University of Pittsburgh in 2009. She received a certificate of professional achievement in narrative medicine from Columbia University in May 2023. She practices full-time as a nurse practitioner in a pediatric endocrinology practice and also works as an adjunct graduate professor with Baylor University. She currently lives in western Pennsylvania with her husband and their children. This is her first collection of poetry.